The Maltese Falcon

Edited by Richard J. Anobile

MACMILLAN

A DARIEN HOUSE BOOK

Pictures and dialogue from the feature motion picture
THE MALTESE FALCON are reproduced in this book by
permission of United Artists Television, Inc. and
Rastar Pictures, Inc.

The motion picture THE MALTESE FALCON
© Copyright 1941 by Warner Bros. Pictures, Inc.
Copyright Renewed 1969.

© 1974, Darien House, Inc.

SBN 333 17347 3

First published in Great Britain in 1974 by
MACMILLAN LONDON LIMITED
London and Basingstoke
Associated companies in New York Dublin
Melbourne Johannesburg & Delhi
In association with Pan Books Ltd.

Printed in the U.S.A.

Introduction

By now I've screened THE MALTESE FALCON over a hundred times and I've lost track of the additional times I've gone over just specific scenes. Through that many viewings one can't help but form impressions of the way John Huston shot the film, the camera angles he chose and the choreography of the actors.

One usually expects experimentation from a director's first film; this *is* Huston's first try at direction. But one also expects quality to be sacrificed for flashy camera action that interferes with the story. Not so here. Despite the talkiness of the film — and there is a great deal of dialogue, more than in the average feature, Huston rivets the viewer to the screen with constant intercuts and a mobile camera. The audience never suspects that the film is devoid of action and that most of the story unfolds through a series of long conversations. The film seemingly moves along at a rapid pace, the viewer never realizing he's been glued to his seat for 100 minutes. It's because of this that I am all the more apprehensive about this first volume in The Film Classics Library.

Although I had previously used the frame blow-up technique in the presentation of comedy film books, most notably a collection of scenes from the Marx Bros. films titled "Why a Duck?", these had been bits and pieces of various films, without the need of continuity and sustaining interest. But now a book had to be devoted entirely to a single film — and it would have to be meaningful and entertaining. The uniqueness of this new series lies in

the fact that every scene and camera setup, as well as every word of dialogue, is recreated to give as permanent and complete a record of the film as it is possible in book form. However, now that I can look at the final product, I am satisfied that the basic objectives have been realized and I will leave it to the reader to decide if he agrees.

The presentation of a film in this manner has, I feel, two valid purposes. The first is sheer entertainment. Fans of this film have only to flip through the pages of the book to relive the memorable dialogue and gripping suspense of the movie at a pace selected by the reader. I personally enjoyed reading and rereading the conversations between Spade and Gutman.

There is a second and more important purpose: This book and the others that will follow, give the serious film student a rare opportunity to closely examine the work of some of our finest directors. Since every camera setup is here, a student interested in film direction will be able to see exactly why Huston did what he did within each scene. Spade's first meeting with Gutman is a classic example of how Huston directs a viewer's attention to his subject and creates an impression of the character. He literally fills the screen with Gutman's bulky figure by shooting from a purposely low angle. In addition to direction, a student may also dwell upon set decoration, lighting and even an actor's stage presence.

The film speaks for itself and critics have already hashed and rehashed its artistic merits. So let me just note a few facts about the film which might be of interest. This version of THE MALTESE FALCON was produced at Warner Bros. in 1941, and is the third filming of Dashiell Hammett's novel of the same name. The first version was filmed in 1931 and starred Bebe Daniels and Riccardo Cortez. It was directed by Roy del Ruth. The second version was titled SATAN WAS A LADY and was filmed in 1936. It was directed by William Dieterle, and starred Bette Davis and Warren Williams, and bore little resemblance to Hammett's story.

It is generally acknowledged that with his portrayal of Sam Spade in this version, Humphrey Bogart solidly established himself as a full-fledged star of the American screen. Stage actor Sydney Greenstreet, who portrays Kaspar Gutman, made his screen debut in this film. He was 61 years old and was nominated for an Academy Award for his performance.

A quick reading of the novel reveals some interesting points about the film. For one thing, Huston, who also wrote the screenplay, saw fit to eliminate at least one character: In the novel Gutman had a daughter. The film censors much of Hammett's original intent. The blame for this most certainly rests with film industry heads who allowed themselves to be intimidated by government and religious censors. We can see a recurrence of this mentality cropping up again today.

Nevertheless, in Hammett's book, Cairo (Peter Lorre) is quite obviously taken with Wilmer (Elisha Cook, Jr.). This is hardly hinted at in the film. Also in the book, Spade completely strips Brigid (Mary Astor) in search of the thousand dollars palmed by Gutman, but not here. And Spade's relationships with Brigid and his secretary can only be left to our imagination which, fortunately, cannot be censored.

Another difference is that at the end of the novel we learn that Gutman was killed by Wilmer. This is clearly not the case in the film. Warner Bros. had originally envisioned a sequel to THE MALTESE FALCON but, alas, it never materialized. Too bad, it could have been fun.

—Richard J. Anobile
New York City
January 1974

Note to reader:

In keeping as true to the film as possible I have left in lap dissolves and fades where I felt they were necessary. The effect of a lap dissolve to the reader will be the appearance of two seemingly superimposed photos. The purpose here – as it was the director's, is to bridge the time and place gap between two scenes.

You will also notice a fuzziness in some frames. This is due to the fact that every photo is taken from blow-ups of the film itself. All possible means have been taken to insure clarity but inconsistencies in negative quality account for the variations of photo densities you will observe.

Acknowledgments

I take this opportunity to thank those individuals and organizations whose cooperation have made this book possible. Rights to produce this book were granted to us by Rastar Pictures, Inc. and United Artists Television, Inc., and I would especially like to acknowledge the assistance of Mr. Phil Feldman and Mr. Ray Stark of Rastar, and of Mr. Jack Benjamin, Mr. Barton Farber and Ms. Eve Baer of UA for their cooperation in seeing to it that all the necessary print and negative materials were made available to us.

Alyne Model and George Norris of Riverside Film Associates transferred my marks to the negative material and attended to the nitty-gritty of that highly technical job. All the blowups were produced by Vita Print.

Harry Chester Associates was responsible for the design.

—Richard J. Anobile

"THE MALTESE FALCON"

With
HUMPHREY BOGART
MARY ASTOR
GLADYS GEORGE
PETER LORRE

and
BARTON MacLANE
LEE PATRICK
SYDNEY GREENSTREET
WARD BOND
JEROME COWAN
A Warner Bros.~First National Picture

Director of Photography ARTHUR EDESON, A.S.C.
Dialogue Director...... ROBERT FOULK
Film Editor ...... THOMAS RICHARDS
Art Director........ ROBERT HAAS
Sound by..... OLIVER S. GARRETSON
Gowns by........... ORRY-KELLY
Makeup Artist...... PERC WESTMORE
Music by........ ADOLPH DEUTSCH
Musical Director ...LEO F. FORBSTEIN

Executive Producer
HAL B. WALLIS

Associate Producer
HENRY BLANKE

Screen Play by
JOHN HUSTON

Based upon the Novel by
DASHIELL HAMMETT

Directed by
JOHN HUSTON

In 1539 the Knight Templars of Malta, paid tribute to Charles V of Spain, by sending him a Golden Falcon encrusted from beak to claw with rarest jewels ----- but pirates seized the galley carrying this priceless token and the fate of the Maltese Falcon remains a mystery to this day---

SAN FRANCISCO

Spade: Yes, sweetheart?
Effie: There's a girl who wants to see you. Her name's Wonderly.
Spade: A customer?

Effie: I guess so. You'll want to see her, anyway. She's a knockout.

Spade: Shoo her in, Effie, darling, Shoo her in!

Effie: . . . Will you come in, Miss Wonderly?

Brigid: . . . Thank you.

Spade: Won't you sit down, Miss Wonderly?

Brigid: Thank you, I inquired at the hotel for the name of a reliable, private detective. They mentioned yours.

Spade: Suppose you tell me about it from the very beginning.
Brigid: I'm from New York.
Spade: Uh-huh.

Brigid: I'm trying to find my sister. I have reason to believe that she's here in San Francisco with a man by the name of Thursby, Floyd Thursby.

Brigid: I don't know where she met him. We've never been as close as sisters ought to be. If we had, perhaps Corinne would have told me that she was planning on running away with him.

Brigid: Mother and Father are in Honolulu. It will kill them. I've got to find her before they get back home. They're coming home the first of the month.

Spade: You've had word of your sister?
Brigid: A letter from her about two weeks ago.

Brigid: It said nothing except that she was all right.
I sent her a telegram begging her to come home.
I sent it to the general delivery here. That was the
only address she gave me.

Brigid: I waited a week and no answer came so I
decided to come out here myself. I wrote her that
I was coming. I shouldn't have done that, should I?

Spade: Oh, it's not always easy to know what to do.
You haven't found her?

Brigid: No. I told her in my letter that I'd be at
the St. Mark and for her to meet me there. I waited
three whole days. She didn't come. She didn't
even send a message. It was horrible.

Brigid: Waiting! I sent her another letter to general
delivery. Yesterday afternoon I went to the post
office. Corinne didn't call for her mail, but Floyd
Thursby did. He wouldn't tell me where Corinne was.

Brigid: He said she didn't want to see me. I can't believe that. He promised to bring her to the hotel if she would come this evening. He said he knew she wouldn't. He promised to come himself if she didn't. He ———————

Archer: Oh, excuse me.

Spade: . . . Oh, its all right, Miles. Come in. Miss Wonderly, my partner, Miles Archer.

Spade: Miss Wonderly's sister ran away from New York with a fellow named Floyd Thursby. They're here in San Francisco.

Spade: Miss Wonderly has seen Thursby and has a date to meet him tonight. Maybe he'll bring the sister with him. The chances are he won't.

Spade: Miss Wonderly wants us to find the sister, get her away from him and back home. Right?
Brigid: Yes.

Spade: Now, it's, er, simply a matter of having a man at the hotel this evening to shadow him when he leads us to your sister.

Spade: If, after we've found her, she still won't leave him, well, we have ways of managing that
Archer: Yeah.

Brigid: Oh, but you must be careful. I'm deathly afraid of him. What he might do. She's so young.

Brigid: And his bringing her here from New York is such a serious——— Mightn't he, mightn't he do something to her?

Spade: Now, just leave that to us. We'll know how to handle him.

Brigid: Oh, but I want you to know he's a dangerous man. I honestly don't think he'd stop at anything. I don't think he'd hesitate to kill Corinne if it would save him.

Archer: Could he cover up by marrying her?
Brigid: He has a wife and three children in England.

Spade: Yes, they usually do, though not always in England.

Spade: What does he look like?

Brigid: He has dark hair and, er, thick, bushy eyebrows. He talks in a loud, blustery manner. He gives the impression of being a violent person. He was wearing a light gray suit and a, a gray hat when I saw him this morning.

Spade: What does he do for a living?
Brigid: Why, I haven't the faintest idea.
Spade: What time's he comin' to see you?
Brigid: After eight oclock.

Spade: All right, Miss Wonderly. We'll have a man there.

Archer: I'll look after it, myself!

Brigid: Oh, thank you. . . .

Brigid: Er, oh, yes.

Brigid: . . . Will that be enough?

Brigid: . . . Thank you.
Spade: Not at all. Oh, it'll help some if you meet Thursby in the lobby.
Brigid: I will.

Archer: Er, you don't have to look for me! I'll see you all right!

Brigid: Thank you. . . . Thank you so much.   **Spade:** Good-bye.   **Archer:** . . . They're right enough. They have brothers in her bag.

Spade: What do you think of her?
Archer: Oh, she's sweet. Maybe you saw her first. Sam, but I spoke first.
Spade: You've got brains. Yes, you——— have.

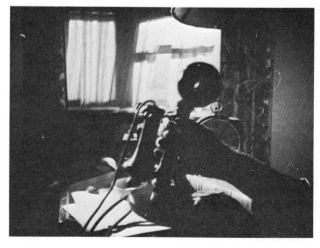

Spade: . . . Hello . . . Yeh. Speaking . . . Miles Archer dead? Where? . . . Bush and Stockton? Yeah . . . In fifteen minutes . . . Thanks.

Spade: . . . Hello, Effie. It's me. . . . Now listen, precious. Miles has been shot . . . Yeah, dead. Now, don't get excited. . . . . Yeah. . . . Um-huh.

Spade: Er, you'll break the news to Iva. I'd fry first. And keep her away from me . . . That's a good girl. Now, get right over there . . . You're an angel! Good-bye.

Policeman: What do you want here?
Spade: Oh, I'm Sam Spade. Tom Polhaus called me.

Policeman: Oh, I didn't know you at first. They're back there.

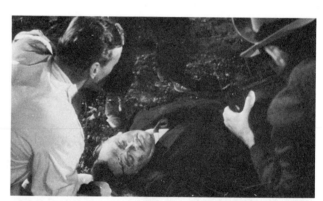

Polhaus: Hello, Sam. I figured you'd want to see it before we took him away.
Spade: Well, thanks, Tom. What happened?

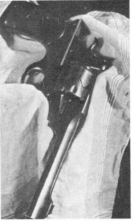

Polhaus: Got him right through the pump with this. It's a Webley. English, ain't it?

Spade: Yeh. A Webley-Forsby forty-five automatic, eight shot. They don't make 'em any more. How many gone out of it?
Polhaus: Just one.

Spade: Let's see. Er, shot up here, huh? Standing like you are, with his back to the fence. The man who shot him stood here. Went over backwards, takin' the top o' the fence with him, and went on down the hill and got caught on that rock. That it?

Polhaus: That's it. The blast burnt his coat.
Spade: Who found him?
Polhaus: Man on the beat.

Spade: Anybody hear the shot?
Polhaus: Well, somebody must've. We just got here. You wanta go down and have a look at him before we take him away?

Spade: No. You've seen everything I could.

Polhaus: His gun was still tucked away on his hip. Hadn't been fired. His overcoat was buttoned. I found a hundred dollar bill in his vest pocket and thirty some bucks in his pants. Was he workin', Sam? Well?

Spade: Yeh. He was tailing a guy named Thursby.
Polhaus: What for? What for?

Spade: We wanted to find out where he lived. Don't crowd me, Tom.

Spade: I'm goin' on down and break the news to Miles' wife.

Polhaus: Gee, it's tough, him gettin' it like that, ain't it? Miles had his faults, just like any of the rest of us, but I guess he must o' had some good points, too, huh?

Spade: I guess so.

Spade: Miss Wonderly, please . . . Checked out? . . .
What time? Oh . . . Any forwarding address? . . .
Thanks.

Spade: Oh, hello, Tom. Hello Lieutenant,

Sam: Come in. Sit down. Drink?

Polhaus: D'you, er, break the news to Miles' wife,
Spade: Uh-huh.
Polhaus: How'd she take it?

Spade: I don't know anything about women.
Polhaus: Humph! Since when?
Dundy: What kind of a gun do you carry?
Spade: None. I don't like 'em. 'Course there are some at the office.

Dundy: You don't happen to have one here? You sure about that?
Spade: Look around. Turn the dump upside down, if if you want to. I won't squawk, if yuh got a search warrant.

Polhaus: Now, we don't wanta make any trouble —
Spade: What're you birds suckin' around here for? Tell me or get out!

Polhaus: Well, you can't treat us like that, Sam. It ain't right. We got our work to do.

Dundy: Why were you tailin' Thursby?

Spade: I wasn't. Miles was. And for the simple reason we had a client that———
Dundy: Who's this client?
Spade: Sorry. I can't tell yuh that.

Polhaus: Be reasonable, Sam. Give us a break, will yuh? How we gonna turn up anything on Miles' killing, if you don't tell us what yuh got?

Dundy: Tom says you were in too much of a hurry to even stop and take a look at your dead partner. And you didn't go to Archer's house to tell his wife.

Dundy: We called your office and the girl there said you told her to do it.

Dundy: I'll give yuh ten minutes to get to a phone and do your talkin' to the girl. I'll give yuh ten minutes to get to Thursby's joint, Geary and Leavenworth. You could do it easily in that time.

Spade: What's your boy friend gettin' at, Tom?

Dundy: Just this: Thursby was shot down in front of his hotel about a half an hour after you left Bush Street.

Spade: Keep your paws off me!

Dundy: What time did you get home?
Spade: Just a few minutes ahead o' you. I was walkin' around thinkin' things over.

Dundy: We knew you weren't here. We tried to get you on the phone. Where did you walk to?

Spade: Out Bush Street.
Dundy: Did you see anybody?
Spade: No. No witnesses. Well, I know where I stand now.

Spade: Sorry I got up on my hind legs, boys, but you fellows tryin' to rope me, made me nervous. Miles gettin' bumped off upset me, and then you birds crackin' foxy. But it's all right now. Now that I know what it's all about.

Polhaus: Oh, forget it, Sam.
Spade: Thursby die?
Polhaus: Yep.
Spade: How'd I kill him? I forget.

Polhaus: He was shot in the back four times with a forty-four or forty-five from across the street. Nobody saw it, but that's how it figures.
Spade: Hotel people know anything about him?
Polhaus: Nothin' except that he lived there a week.

Spade: Alone?
Polhaus: Yeh, alone.
Spade: Did you find out who he was? What his game was? Well, did yuh?

Dundy: We thought you could tell us that.
Spade: I've never seen Thursby, dead or alive.
Dundy: Well, you know me, Spade. If yuh did it, or if yuh didn't, you'll get a square deal from me, and most of the breaks.

Dundy: Don't know as I'd blame yuh much; a man that killed your partner, but that won't stop me from nailin' yuh.

Spade: Fair enough.

Spade: But I'd feel better about it if you'd have a drink with me.

Spade: Success to crime!

Effie: She's in there.

Spade: I told you to keep her away from me.

Effie: Yes, but you didn't tell me how. Oh, don't be cranky with me, Sam. I've had her all night.

Spade: Sorry, angel. I didn't mean———

Spade: Hello, Iva.

Iva: Oh, Sam!

Spade: Darling. Effie take care of everything?

Iva: I think so. Sam, did you kill him?

Spade: Who put that bright idea in your head?

Iva: Well, I thought you said if it wasn't for Miles, you'd———

Iva: Be kind to me, Sam.

Spade: You killed my husband, Sam. Be kind to me!

Spade: Don't Iva. Don't. You shouldn't have come here today, darling. You ought to be home.

Iva: You'll come soon?
Spade: Soon as I can.

Spade: Good-bye, Iva.

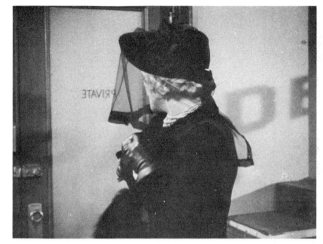

Effie: Well, how did you and the widow make out?

Spade: She thinks I shot Miles.
Effie: So you could marry her?

Spade: The cops think I killed Thursby, the guy Miles was tailing for that Wonderly dame.

Spade: Who do you think I shot?

Effie: Are you going to marry Iva?

Spade: Aw, don't be silly. I wish I'd never laid eyes on her.

Spade: You're an angel: a nice, rattle-brained, little angel.
Effie: Oh, am I?
Spade: Thanks, honey.

Effie: Suppose I told you that your Iva hadn't been home many minutes, when I arrived to break the news at three o'clock this morning?

Spade: Are you telling me?

Effie: She kept me waiting at the door, while she undressed.

Effie: Her clothes were on a chair, where she'd dump them, hat and coat underneath.

Effie: Her slip, on top, was still warm. She'd wrinkled up the bed, but the wrinkles weren't mashed down.

Spade: You're a detective, darling, but she didn't kill him.

Effie: Do the police really think you shot this what's-his-name? Do they? Look at me, Sam. You worry me.

Effie: You always think you know what you're doing, but you're too slick for your own good. Some day you're going to find it out.

Effie: Spade and Archer. Oh, yes, Miss Wonderly.

Spade: Hello. Yeh, this is Sam Spade.

Spade: Er, where? Coronet Apartments, California Avenue, apartment 1001. What's the name?

Spade: Miss LeBlanc. Okay, I'll be right over.

Spade: Oh, er, have Miles' desk moved out of the office and have Spade and Archer taken off all the doors and, er, have Samuel Spade put on.

Brigid: Oh, come in, Mr. Spade.

Brigid: Oh, er, everything's upside down. I haven't finished unpacking.

Brigid: Mr. Spade, I — I have a terrible, terrible confession to make.

Brigid: Sit down.

Brigid: That story I told you yesterday was just a story.

Spade: Oh, that we — didn't exactly believe your story, Miss, er, ——————

Spade: What is your name, Wonderly or LeBlanc?

Brigid: It's really O'Shaughnessy, Brigid O'Shaughnessy.
Spade: We didn't exactly believe your story, Miss O'Shaughnessy. We believed your two hundred dollars.

Brigid: You mean that——————
Spade I mean you paid us——————
——————more than if you'd been telling us the truth and enough more to make it all right.

Brigid: Tell me, Mr. Spade, am I to blame for for last night?

Spade: Well, you warned us that Thursby was dangerous. Of course, you lied to us about your sister and all that, but that didn't count. We didn't believe yuh. Na, — wouldn't say that you were at fault.

Brigid: Thank you. Mr. Archer was so alive yesterday; so solid and hearty, and———

Spade: Stop it! He knew what he was doing. Those are the chances we take.

Brigid: Was he married?

Spade: Yeh, with ten thousand insurance, no children, and a wife that didn't like him.

Brigid: Please don't.

Spade: Well, that's the way it was. Anyway, there's no time for worrying about that now.

Spade: Out there's a flock o' policemen and assistant district attorneys running around with their noses to the ground.

Brigid: Mr. Spade, do they know about me?
Spade: Not yet. I've been stalling 'em, until I could see yuh.
Brigid: Do they have to know about me?

Brigid: I mean, can't you shield me so that I won't have to answer their questions?
Spade: Maybe, but I gotta know what its all about.

Brigid: I can't tell you. I cant tell you now. I will later, when I can.

Brigid: You've got to trust me, Mr. Spade. Oh, I — I'm so alone and afraid.

Brigid: I've got nobody to help me, if you won't help me.

Brigid: Be generous, Mr. Spade. You're brave. You're strong. You can spare me some of that courage and strength, surely. Help me, Mr. Spade.

Brigid: I need help so badly. I've no right to ask you, I know I haven't, but I do ask you. Help me.

Spade: You won't need much of anybody's help. You're good.

Spade: It's chiefly your eyes, I think, and that throb you get in your voice when you say things like "Be generous, Mr. Spade."

Brigid: I deserve that.

Brigid: But the lie was in the way I said it: Not at all in what I said. It's my fault, if you can't believe me now.

Spade: Ah. Now, you are dangerous.

Spade: Well, I'm afraid I'm — I'm not gonna be able to be of much help to yuh, unless I've got some idea what it's all about.

Spade: For instance, I've gotta have some sort of a line on your Floyd Thursby.

Brigid: I met him in the Orient. We came here from Hong Kong last week. He promised to help me. He took advantage of my dependence on him to betray me.
Spade: Betray yuh? How? Why did you want him shadowed?
Brigid: I wanted to find out how far he'd gone, whom he was meeting: Things like that.

Spade: Did he kill Archer?
Brigid: Certainly. He had a Luger in his shoulder holster.
Spade: Archer wasn't shot with a Luger.
Brigid: Mr. Spade, you don't think I had anything to do with the death of Mr. Archer?
Spade: Did yuh?

Brigid: No.
Spade: That's good.
Brigid: Floyd always carried an extra revolver in his overcoat pocket.
Spade: Well, why all the guns?

Brigid: He lived by them. The story in Hong Kong is that he first came to the Orient as bodyguard to a gambler whc'd had to leave the States. The gambler had since disappeared and Floyd knew about the disappearance.

Brigid: I don't know. I do know he always went to sleep without covering the floor around his bed with crumpled newspapers, so that nobody could come silently into his room.

Spade: Well, you picked a nice sort of a playmate.
Brigid: Only that sort could have helped me, if he'd been loyal.

49

Spade: How bad a spot are you actually in?
Brigid: As bad as could be.

Spade: Physical danger?

Brigid: I'm not heroic. I don't think there's anything worse than death.

Spade: Then, it's that?
Brigid: It's that, as surely as we're sitting here, unless you help me.

Spade: Who killed Thursby, your enemies, or his?
Brigid: I don't know. His, I suppose. I'm afraid. I — I don't know.

Spade: Ah, this is hopeless!

Spade: I don't know what you want done!

Spade: I don't even know if you know what you want done.

Brigid: You won't go to the police!

Spade: Go to them? All I gotta do is stand still, and they'll be swarming all over me. All right, I'll tell 'em all I know, and you'll have to take your chances.

Brigid: You've been patient with me. You've tried to help me. It's useless and hopeless, I suppose. I do thank you for what you've done.

Brigid: I'll have to take my chances.

Spade: How much money have yuh got?

Brigid: I've got about five hundred dollars left.

Spade: Give it to me.

Spade: There's only four hundred here.

Brigid: Why, I had to keep some to live on.
Spade: Well, can't yuh get some more?

Brigid: No.
Brigid: I've got some furs and a little jewelry.
Spade: You'll have to hock 'em.

Spade: There yuh are. I'll be back as soon as I can with the best news I can manage, I'll ring four times; long, short, long, short.

Spade: And, oh, you needn't bother to come to the door, I'll let myself in.

Spade: Anything stirring. Did you send the flowers?

Spade: You're invaluable, darling. Say, get my lawyer on the phone, will yuh?

Spade: Hello, Sid? . . . I think I'm going to have to tell a coroner to go to blazes, Sid . . . Say, can I hide behind the sanctity of my client's identity, secrets and what-nots all the same, priest or lawyer?

Spade: Yeh, I know, but Dundy's getting a little rambunctious, and maybe it is a bit thick this time. Yeh. What'll it cost to be on the safe side? . . . Well, maybe it's worth it. Okay, go ahead.

Effie: Gardenia.

Spade: Quick, darling, in with him!

Effie: Will you come in, ———
——— Mr. Cairo?

Spade: Will you sit down, Mr. ———
——— Cairo?

Cairo: Thank you, sir.

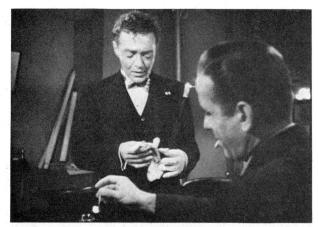

Spade: Now, what can I do for you, Mr. Cairo?

Cairo: May a stranger offer condolences for your partner's unfortunate death?
Spade: Thanks.

Cairo: Is there, Mr. Spade, as the newspapers imply, a certain relationship between that, er, unfortunate happening and, er, the death a little later of the man Thursby?

Cairo: I beg your pardon. No. More than idle curiosity prompted my question. See, Mr. Spade, I'm trying to recover an ornament that, er, shall we say, has been mislaid?
Spade: Uh-huh.

Cairo: I thought and hoped you could assist me. The ornament, er, is a statuette, black figure of a bird.

Cairo: I am prepared to pay, on behalf of the ————

Cairo: ———— figure's rightful owner, the sum of five thousand dollars for its recovery.

Cairo: I am prepared to promise that, er, what is the phrase, er, "No questions will be asked."

Spade: Five thousand dollars is a lot o' money.

Spade: Yes, Effie?

Effie: Is there anything else?
Spade: No, that'll be all. Just be sure to lock the door behind yuh on your way out. Good night.

Spade: Five thousand dollars is a ⸺

Cairo: You will clasp your hands together at the back of your neck?

Cairo: I intend to ——— search your offices, Mr. Spade.

Cairo: I warn you, if you attempt to prevent me, I shall certainly shoot you.
Spade: Go ahead and search.

Cairo: You will please come to the center of the room? I have to make certain that you are not armed.

 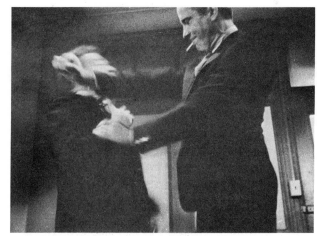

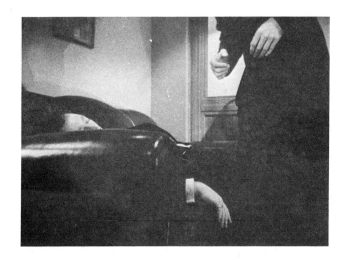 

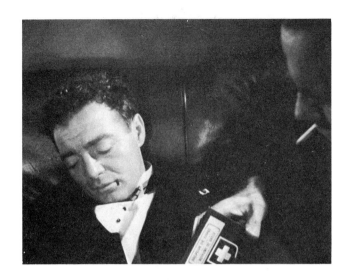

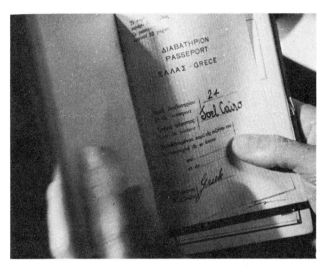

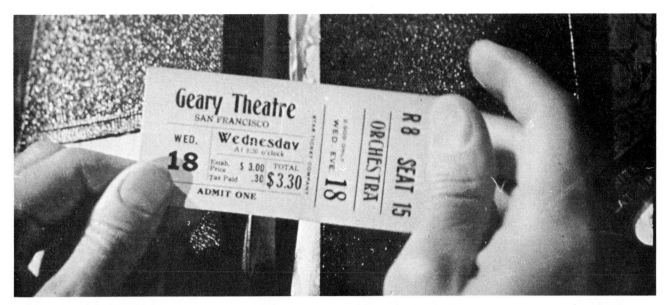

Cairo: Look what you did to my shirt!

Spade: Sorry. But imagine my embarrassment when I found out that five thousand dollar offer was just hooey.

Cairo: Mr. Spade, my offer is genuine. I am prepared to pay five thousand dollars for the figure's return.

Cairo: You have it?
Spade: No.

Cairo: But if it isn't here, why did you risk serious injury to prevent my searching for it?

Spade: Why, I should sit around here and let people come in and stick me up! Huh!

Cairo: Certainly it is only natural that I try to save the owner such a considerable expense, if possible.

Spade: Who is he?
Cairo: Mr. Spade, you'll forgive my not answering that question.

Spade: Yeh. Well, I think we'd be better off all around if we'd put our cards on the table.
Cairo: No. I do not think it would be better.

Cairo: You see, Mr. Spade, er, if you know more than I do, then I shall profit by your knowledge. So will you, to the extent of five thousand dollars.

Spade: Oh, there's nothing like five thousand dollars here.

Cairo: Oh, you want some assurance of my sincerity? A retainer? Would that do?
Spade: It might.

Cairo: Er, you will take, say, one hundred dollars?
Spade: No. I will take, say, two hundred dollars.

Spade: Now, let's see. Your first guess was that I had the bird. There's nothing to that. What's your second guess?
Cairo: That you know where it is, or, at least, you know it is where you can get it.

Spade: You're not hiring me to do any murders or burglaries, but simply to get it back, if possible, in an honest, lawful way?
Cairo: Er, if possible. But, er, in any case, with discretion.

Cairo: When you wish to contact me, sir, I'm staying at the Hotel Belvedere, room 635.

Cairo: I sincerely expect the greatest mutual benefit from our association, Mr. Spade.

Cairo: Oh, may I please have my gun now?

Spade: Oh, sure. I'd forgotten all about it.

Cairo: You will please clasp your hands together at the back of your neck.

Cairo: I intend to search your offices.

Spade: Well, I'll be ——— Why, sure. G-g-go ahead. I won't stop you.

Spade: Turn to the right, and go up the hill, Driver.
Driver: Okay.

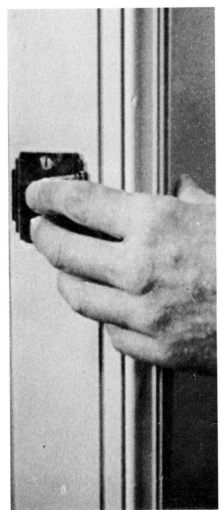

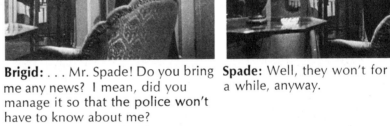

Brigid: . . . Mr. Spade! Do you bring me any news? I mean, did you manage it so that the police won't have to know about me?

Spade: Well, they won't for a while, anyway.

Brigid: Oh, you are wonderful! You won't get into any trouble, will you?
Spade: I don't mind a reasonable amount of trouble.

Brigid: Er, do sit down.

Spade: . . . You, er ——— You aren't exactly the sort of a person you pretend to be, are yuh?

Brigid: Why! I, I'm not sure I know exactly what you mean.

Spade: The school girl manner. You know, blushing, stammering and all that.

Brigid: I haven't lived a good life. I've been bad. Worse than you could know.

Spade: Yeah. That's good, because if you actually were as innocent as you pretend to be, we'd never get anywhere.

Brigid: I won't be innocent.

Spade: Good. Oh, er, by the way, I saw Joel Cairo tonight.

Brigid: Do you know him?

Spade: Only slightly.

Spade: You're good. You're very good.

Brigid: What did he say?

Spade: About what?
Brigid: About me.
Spade: Nothing.
Brigid: What did you talk about then?

Spade: He offered me five thousand dollars for the black bird.

Spade: Er, er, you, you're not gonna go around the room straightening things and poking the fire again, are yuh?

Brigid: No, I'm not. What did you say?

Spade: I said five thousand dollars was a lot of money.

Brigid: It 'tis. It's more than I can ever offer you if I have to bid for your loyalty.
Spade: That's good coming from you.

Spade: What have you ever given me besides money?

Spade: Have you ever given me any of your confidence, any of the truth?

Spade: Haven't you tried to buy my loyalty with money and nothing else?

Brigid: What else is there I can buy you with?

Spade: . . . I don't care what your secrets are. But I can't go ahead without more confidence in you than I've got now.

Spade: You've got to convince me that you know what this is all about, that you aren't just fiddling around.

Spade: Hoping it'll all come out right in the end.

Brigid: Can't you trust me a little longer?

Spade: Well, how much is a little? What are you waiting for?
Brigid: Why, I've got to talk to Joel Cairo.

Spade: You can see him tonight. He's at the theatre. It'll be out soon.

Spade: I'll leave a message at his hotel.
Brigid: But he can't come here. I can't let him know where I am. I'm afraid.
Spade: My place then.

Spade: Hello! I want to leave a message for Joel Cairo.

Brigid: All right. . . . You know I never would
have placed myself in this position if I didn't
trust you completely.
Spade: Huh! That again?

Brigid: . . . You know that's true, though.
Spade: You don't have to trust me as long as you can persuade me to trust you.

Spade: But don't worry about that now. He'll be along any minute.

Spade: You get your business with Cairo over with and then we'll see how we stand.

Brigid: And you'll let me go about it with him ———— in my own way.
Spade: Oh, sure.

Brigid: You are a godsend.

Spade: Oh, now, don't overdo it.

Cairo: . . . Mr. Spade! There is a boy outside. He seems to be watching the house.

Spade: Yeah, I know. I spotted him.

Brigid: What? What's that? What boy?
Spade: I don't know. A kid.

Spade: He's been tailing me all evening.

Brigid: Did he follow you to my apartment?
Spade: No. I shook him long before that. Come in, Mr. Cairo.

Cairo: I'm delighted to see you again, madame.

Brigid: I was sure you would be, Joe.

Brigid: Mr. Spade told me about your offer for the falcon.

Brigid: How soon can you have the money ready?
Cairo: The money is ready.

Brigid: In cash?
Cairo: Oh, yes.
Brigid: You're ready to pay five thousand dollars if we turn over the falcon to you?

Cairo: Excuse me, please. I must have expressed myself badly. I did not mean to say that I have the money in my pocket, but that I am ready to get it for you on a few minutes' notice at any time during banking hours.

Spade: Yes, that's probably true. He only had a couple o' hundred on 'im when I searched him late this afternoon at my office.

Cairo: I shall be able to have the money for you at, say, half-past ten in the morning.

88

Brigid: But I haven't got the falcon. . . . I'll have it in another week at the most, though.
Cairo: Then where is it?

Brigid: Where Floyd hid it.
Cairo: Floyd? Er ——— And you
know where he hid it? Then why
do we have to wait a week?

Brigid: Oh, perhaps not a
whole week.

Cairo: And why if I may ask
another question, are you wiling
to sell it to me?

Brigid: Because, I'm afraid. After
what happened to Floyd I'm afraid
to touch it except to turn it over
to somebody else.

Cairo: What exactly did happen to
Floyd?

Brigid: The fat man.

Cairo: The fat man? Is he here?

Brigid: I don't know. I suppose so. What difference does it make?

Cairo: It might make a world of difference.

Brigid: Or you or me ———

Cairo: Precisely. But, er, shall we add, more certainly, the boy outside?

Brigid: Yes. But you might be able to get around him, Joel, as you did the one in Istanbul! What was his name?

Cairo: You mean the one you couldn't get to come to ————

Cairo: This is the second time that you laid hands on me!

Spade: When you're slapped you'll take it and like it.

Brigid: Who's that?

Spade: I don't know. Be quiet. . . .

Spade: Er, hello. Well, you guys pick swell hours to do your visiting in. What is it this time?

Dundy: We want to talk to you, Spade.
Spade: Well, go ahead and talk.

Polhaus: We don't have to do it out here in the hall, do we, Sam?
Spade: You can't come in.

Polhaus: Oh, come off it now, Sam.

Spade: You aren't tryin' to strong-arm me, are you, Tom?
Polhaus: Why don't you be reasonable?

Dundy: It would pay you to play along with us a little, Spade. You got away with this and you got away with that. But you can't keep it up forever.
Spade: Stop me when yuh can.
Dundy: That's what I intend to do. There's talk goin' around about you and Archer's wife. Is there anything to it?
Spade: Not a thing.
Dundy: The talk is that she tried to get a divorce from him so she could put in with you, but he wouldn't give it to her. Anything to that?
Spade: No.
Dundy: There's even talk that that's why he was put on the spot.

Spade: Oh, don't be a hog, Dundy. Your first idea that I killed Thursby because he killed Miles, falls to pieces if you blame me for killing Miles, too.
Dundy: You haven't heard me say you killed anybody. You're the one that keeps bringing that up.
Spade: Say, haven't you anything better to do than to keep popping in here early every morning asking a lot o' fool questions?
Dundy: Yeh, an' gettin' a lot o' lyin' answers.
Spade: Take it easy.
Dundy: If you say there's nothin' between you and Archer's wife you're a liar and I'm tellin' you so.
Spade: Is that the hot tip that brought you up here at this ungodly hour of the night.
Dundy: That's one of 'em.
Spade: And the other?
Dundy: Let us in! . . . All right, Spade, we'll go. Maybe you're right in buckin' us. Think it over.

Cairo: Help!

Dundy: I guess we're goin' in.
Spade: I guess you are.

Dundy: Here, what's goin' on in here?

Cairo: Look! Look! Look, officer! Look what she did!

Dundy: Did you do that?
Brigid: I had to. I was alone in here with him. He tried to attack me. I had to keep him off.

 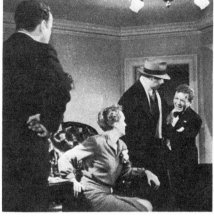 

Brigid: I couldn't bring myself to shoot him!

Cairo: You dirty, filthy liar! You! . . .

Cairo: It isn't true! I came up here in good faith and then both of them attacked me.

Cairo: And then when he went out to talk to you he left her in here with a pistol and she said as soon as you leave they're going to kill me.

Cairo: So I called for help because I didn't want you to leave me and be murdered,

Cairo: And then, then she struck me with the pistol!

Brigid: Why don't you make him tell the truth?

  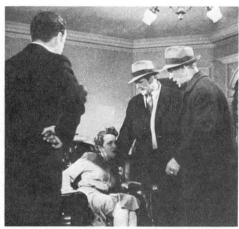

Dundy & Polhaus: Wait a minute! **Polhaus:** That's no way to act! **Dundy:** Well, Tom, I don't guess we'll be wrong runnin' the lot of 'em in.

Spade: Now don't be in a hurry, boys. Everything can be explained.

Dundy: I'll bet.

Spade: Miss O'Shaughnessy, may I present
Lieutenant Dundy and Detective Sergeant Polhaus?
Miss O'Shaughnessy is an operative in my employ.
er, since yesterday.
Cairo: That's a lie, too!

Spade: That is Mr. Joel Cairo.

Spade: Cairo was an acquaintance of Thursby's. He came into my office late this afternoon ———

Spade: ——— and hired me to find something that Thursby was supposed to have on him when he was bumped off. It, er, looked funny to me the way he put it, so I wouldn't touch it.

Spade: Then he pulled a gun on me. Well, that's neither here nor there unless we start preferring charges against each other.

Spade: Well, anyway, Miss O'Shaughnessy and I discussed the matter and we decided to find out exactly how much he knew about Miles' and Thursby's killings so we asked him to come up here.

Spade: Now maybe we did put the questions to him a little roughly, er ——— You know how that is, Lieutenant? But, er, we didn't hurt him enough to make him cry for help.

Dundy: Well, what have yuh got to say to that?
Cairo: I don't know what to say.
Dundy: Try tellin' the facts.

Cairo: What? Facts?
Dundy: Aw, quit stallin'. All yuh have to do is swear out a complaint they took a poke at yuh and I'll throw 'em in the can.

Spade: Go ahead, Cairo. Tell him you'll do it.
Then we'll swear out a complaint against you and
he'll have the lot of us.
Dundy: Get your hats.

Spade: Well, boys and girls, we put it over nicely!

Dundy: Go on, get your hats!

Spade: Aw, don't yuh know when you're bein'
kidded?
Dundy: No, but that can wait till we get down to
the hall.

Spade: Aw, wake up, Dundy, you're being kidded!

Spade: When I heard the buzzer I said to Miss O'Shaughnessy and Cairo here, I said: "There's the police again. They're getting to be a nuisance!"

Spade: "When you hear them going, one o' you scream and then we'll see how far along we can string 'em, until they tumble."

Polhaus: Stop it, Sam!

Dundy: That cut on his head. How did that get there?
Spade: Ask him. Maybe he cut himself shaving.

Cairo: The cut. No. When we pretended to be struggling for the gun, I fell over the carpet. I fell.

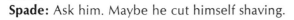

Polhaus: Aw, horse feathers!
Dundy: Take him along, anyway, for packin' a gun.

Spade: Aw, don't be a sap. That gun was a plant. It was one o' mine.

Spade: Too bad it was only a twenty-five, or maybe you could prove that was the gun that Miles and Thursby were shot with.

Polhaus: No, Sam! No!
Spade: Well, then, get him out o' here!

Dundy: Get their names and addresses.
Cairo: My name is Joel Cairo, Hotel Belvedere.
Brigid: I ———
Spade: Miss O'Shaughnessy's address is my office.

Dundy: Where do yuh live?
Spade: Get him out o' here! I've had enough o' this!
Polhaus: Now, now, take it easy, will yuh, Sam?

Polhaus: Is that all yuh want, Lieutenant?
Dundy: Yeah.

Cairo: I think I'll be going now.
Spade: Well, what's the hurry, Cairo?

Cairo: Th-there is no hurry. It's getting quite late, and —

Spade: Tell him to leave the gun.

Polhaus: I hope you know what you're doin', Sam.

Brigid: You're absolutely the wildest, most unpredictable person I've ever known. Do you always carry on so high-handed?

Spade: Well, you've had your talk with Cairo. Now, you can talk to me.

Brigid: Oh, yes, of course.
Spade: I'm listening.

Spade: I'm still listening.
Brigid: Oh, look at the time! I must be going.

Spade: Oh, no. Not till you've told me all about it.

Brigid: Am I a prisoner?
Spade: Maybe the boy outside hasn't gone home yet.

Brigid: Do you suppose he's still there?
Spade: Likely. You can start now.

Brigid: You are the most insistent person.

Spade: And wild and unpredictable, huh? Say, what' this bird, this falcon, that everybody's all steamed up about?

Brigid: Supposing I wouldn't tell you anything about it a'tall? What would you do, something wild and unpredictable?
Spade: I might.

Brigid: It's a black figure, as you know, smooth and shiny, of a bird, a hawk or falcon, about that high.

Spade: Oh, here. Well, what, er, ——— What makes it so important?

Brigid: I don't know, They wouldn't tell me, They offered me five hundred pounds, if I'd help them get it away from the man who had it.

Spade: That was in Istambul?

Brigid: Er, Marmora.
Spade: Go ahead.

Brigid: But that's all. They promised me five hundred pounds if I'd help them, and I did. Then we found out that Joel Cairo intended to desert us, taking the falcon with him, and leaving Floyd and me nothing, so we did exactly that to him.

Brigid: But, then, I wasn't any better off than I was keeping his promise to me ———

Brigid: —— about sharing equally. I'd learned that by the time we got here.

Spade: What's the bird made of?
Brigid: Porcelain or black stone. I don't know. I only saw it once for a few minutes. Floyd showed it to me when we first got hold of it.

Spade: You are a liar!
Brigid: I am. I've always been a liar.

Spade: Well, don't — don't brag about it. Was there any truth at all in that yarn?

Brigid: Some. Not very much.

Spade: Well, we got all night. Coffee'll be ready soon. We'll have a cup and try again.

Brigid: Oh, I'm ——— I'm so tired, so tired of lying and making up lies.

Brigid: Not knowing what is a lie and what's the truth.

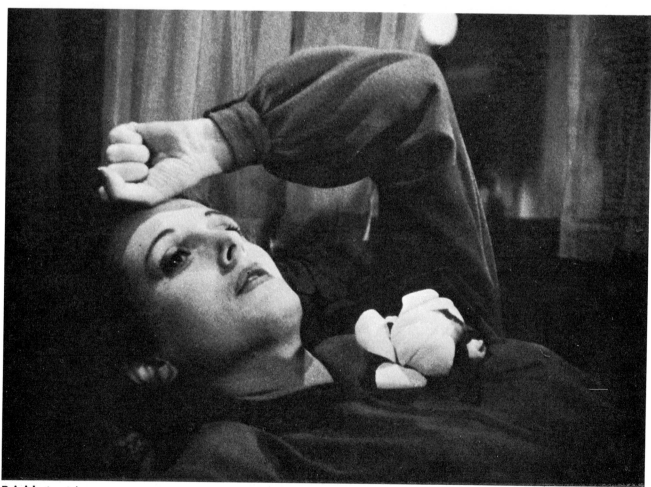

Brigid: I wish ———

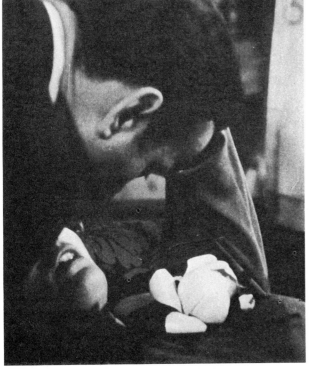

Page Boy: Call for Mr. Mayo!   **Spade:** I wanta talk to Mr. Cairo.

Spade: Joel Cairo.   **Spade:** Oh, thanks.

Spade: Where is he?
Wilmer: What?
Spade: Where is he?
Wilmer: Who?
Spade: Cairo.

Wilmer: What do you think you're doin', Jack? Kiddin' me?
Spade: I'll tell you when I am. New York, aren't yuh?
Wilmer: Shove off.

Spade: You're gonna have to talk to me before you're through, sonny. Some of you will, and you can tell the fat man I said so.

Wilmer: Keep askin' for it and you're gonna get it, plenty. I told you to shove off. Shove off!

Spade: People lose teeth talkin' like that. If you wanta hang around, you'll be polite.

Girl: Luke.

Luke: Hello, Sam,
Spade: Hello, Luke.

Luke: Say, that was too bad about Miles.
Spade: Yeah. It was a tough break. I wanta show you somethin'.

Spade: What do yuh let these cheap gunmen hang around the lobby for, with their heaters bulging in their clothes?

Luke: What do you want here? Well, if you don't want anything, beat it and don't come back!

Wilmer: I won't forget you guys.

Cairo: 603.
Clerk: Yes, sir.

Luke: What is it?
Spade: I don't know, I just spotted him.
Luke: Say, what about Miles?
Spade: I'll see yuh, Luke.

Spade: Good morning.
Cairo: Good morning.
Clerk: Here you are, sir.

Spade: Let's go some place where we can talk.
Cairo' No, no, no. Our private conversations have not been such that I'm anxious to continue them. Forgive my speaking so bluntly, but it is the truth.

Spade: You mean last night? What else could I do? I had to throw in with 'er. I don't know where that bird is. Neither do you. She does. How're we gonna get it if I don't play along with her?
Cairo: You always have a very smooth explanation ready, huh?

Spade: What do you want me to do, learn to stutter? Dundy take you down to the station? How long'd they work on yuh?

Cairo: Till a little while ago.

Spade: What'd they shake out of yuh?

Cairo: Shake out? Not one thing. I adhered to the course you indicated earlier in your rooms, but I certainly wish you would have invented a more reasonable story.

Cairo: I felt distinctly like an idiot repeating it.
Spade: Well, don't worry about the story's goofiness. A sensible one would have had us all in the cooler. You sure you didn't tell 'em anything?

Cairo: I did not.
Spade: Well, you'll want to sleep, if you've been standing up under a police grilling all night. I'll see yuh later.

Effie: Yes, I'll have him call you the minute he comes in. ————— That's the third time she's called this morning. Miss O'Shaughnessy's in there.

Spade: Anything else?
Effie: The District Attorney's Office called. Bryan would like to see you.
Spade: Uh-huh.

Effie: And a Mr. Gutman called. And when I told him you weren't in, he said, "Would you please tell him that the young man gave me his message, and that I phoned, and will phone again?"
Spade: Gutman, huh?

120

Spade: Thanks, darling.

Brigid: Darling! Somebody's been in my apartment! It's all upside down! Every which way! I changed as fast as I could and came right over here. You must have let that boy follow you there.
Spade: Oh, no, angel. I shook him off long before I ever went to your place.

Spade: It might o' been Cairo. He wasn't at the hotel last night. He told me he'd been standing up under a police grilling. I wonder.
Brigid: You saw Joel this morning?
Spade: Yeah.
Brigid: Why?

Spade: Because, my own true love, I've gotta keep in some sort of touch with all the loose ends of this dizzy affair, if I'm ever gonna make heads or tails of it. Now, we've got to find a new home for you.

Brigid: I won't go back there!

Spade: I got an idea. Wait a minute.

Spade: What does your woman's intuition tell you about her?
Effie: She's all right. Oh, maybe it's her own fault for being in whatever the trouble is, but she's all right, if that's what you mean.
Spade: That's what I mean. Are you strong enough for her to put her up for a few days?

Effie: You mean at home?
Spade: Yeh.
Effie: Is she in any danger, Sam?
Spade: I think she is.
Effie: Gee, that'd scare Mom into a green hemmorhage. I'd have to say she's a surprise witness or something you're keeping under cover until the last minute.

Spade: You're a darling.

Spade: Oh, Brigid. Effie here's offered to put you up for a few days.

Brigid: Oh, that's very kind of you.

Spade: You better start now. Go out the back entrance. There's usually a cab parked there by the alleyway. You ride part way with her over to the bridge, and make sure you're not followed.

Spade: You better change cabs a couple o' times, just to be on the safe side.
Effie: I'll give Mom a ring.
Spade: There's time enough for that when yuh get back. I'll call you later.

123

Spade: This is Samuel Spade. Say, my secretary tells me Mr. Bryan wants to see me. Yeh. Yeh. Ask him what time's most convenient to him. Spade. S-p-a-d-e.

Spade: Hello, honey.

Spade: Yeh. Two thirty. All right. Thanks.

Iva: Oh, Sam, forgive me. Please forgive me. I sent those policemen to your place last night.

Iva: I was mad, crazy with jealousy. I phoned them, if they went there, they'd learn something about Miles' murder.
Spade: What made you think of that?

Iva: I was mad, Sam, I wanted to hurt you.
Spade: Did you tell 'em who you were when you phoned?
Iva: Oh, no Sam, dearest, I ——————

Spade: Where'd you phone from?
Iva: The drug store across from your place.

Spade: You better hurry along home and think of something to tell the police. You'll be hearing from them. And, by the way, where were you the night Miles was murdered?

Iva: Home. I was ——————
Spade: No! But, if that's your story, it's all right with me.

Spade: Now, you run along.

Spade: Hello. Yeh, this is Spade.

Spade: Oh, yes, Mr. Gutman, I got it. Yeh. I been waitin' to hear from yuh... Why, not? The sooner, the better. Say fifteen minutes... Right. 12 C.

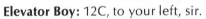

Elevator Boy: 12C, to your left, sir.

Gutman: Ah, Mr. Spade!
Spade: How do you do, Mr. Gutman?

Gutman: You begin well, sir. I distrust a man who says "when."

Gutman: He's got to be careful not to drink too much. It's because he's not to be trusted when he does.

Gutman: Well, sir, here's to plain speaking and clear understanding.

Gutman: You're a close-mouth man?

Spade: No. I like to talk.

Gutman: Better and better. I distrust a close-mouth man.

Gutman: He generally picks the wrong time to talk, and says the wrong things.

Gutman: Talking's something you can't do judiciously, unless you keep in practice.

Gutman: Now, sir. We'll talk, if you like. I'll tell you right out, I'm a man who likes talking to a man who likes to talk.

Spade: Swell! Will we talk about the black bird?

Gutman: H'mm, — H'mm, h'mm.

Gutman: You're the man for me, sir. No beating about the bush. Right to the point. Let's talk about the black bird, by all means. First, sir, answer me a question.

Gutman: Are you here as Miss O'Shaughnessy's representative?
Spade: Well, there's nothing certain either way. It depends.

Gutman: It depends on? Maybe it depends on Joel Cairo.

Spade: Maybe.

Gutman: The question is, then, which you represent. It'll be one or the other.
Spade: I didn't say so.
Gutman: Who else is it?

Spade: There's me.

Gutman: Ah. H'mm, h'mm — h'mm.

Gutnam: That's wonderful, sir, wonderful.

Gutman: I do like a man who tells you right out he's lookin' for himself. Don't we all? I don't trust a man who say's he's not.

Spade: Uh-huh. Now, let's talk about the black bird.

Gutman: Let's. Mr. Spade, have you any conception of how much money can be got for that black bird?
Spade: No.

Gutman: Well, sir, if I told you — if I told you half, you'd call me a liar.

Spade: No, not even if I thought so. But you tell me what it is, and I'll figure out the profit.

Gutman: H'mm, — h'mm, h'mm. You mean, you don't know what that bird is?

Spade: Oh, I know what it's supposed to look like. And I know the value, in human life, you people put on it.

Gutman: She didn't tell you what it is? Cairo didn't, either?

Spade: He offered me ten thousand for it.

Gutman: Ten thousand! Dollars, mind you; not even pounds! Do you know what that bird is, sir? What is your impression?

Spade: Well, there's not very much to go by. Cairo didn't say he did, and he didn't say he didn't.

Spade: She said she didn't, but, er, I took it for granted she was lying.

Gutman: Not an injudicious thing to do.

Gutman: If they don't know I'm the only one in the whole, wide, sweet world who does.

Spade: Swell! When you've told me, that'll make two of us.

Gutman: Mathematically correct, sir, but I don't know for certain that I'm going to tell you.
Spade: Oh, don't be foolish. You know what it is. I know where it is. That's why I'm here,

Gutman: Well, sir, where is it? You see, I must tell you what I know, but you won't tell me what you know. It's hardly equitable, sir.

Gutman: No, no. I don't think we can do business along those lines.

Spade: Well, think again, and think fast! I told that gunsel o' yours you'd have to talk to me before you're through.

Spade: I'm telling yuh now! You'll talk to me today, or you are through!

Spade: What are you wasting my time for?

Spade: I can get along without you!

Spade: And another thing. Keep that gunsel out o' my way while you're makin' up your mind.

Spade: I'll kill 'im, if yuh don't. I'll kill 'im.

Gutman: Well, sir, I must say you have a most violent temper.

Spade: Think it over. You've got till five o'clock.

Then, you're either in, or out ———— for keeps!

Bryan: Who killed Thursby?
Spade: I don't know.
Bryan: Perhaps you don't, but you could make an excellent guess.

142

Spade: My guess might be excellent, or it might be crummy, but Mrs. Spade didn't raise any children dippy enough to make guesses in front of a district attorney, an assistant district attorney and a stenographer.

Bryan: Why shouldn't you, if you've nothing to conceal?

Spade: Everybody has something to conceal?

Bryan: I'm a sworn officer of the law twenty-four hours a day, and neither formality nor informality justifies you. withholding evidence of crime from me **except,** of course, on constitutional grounds.

Spade: Now, both you and the police have as much as accused me of being mixed up in the other night's murders. Well, I've had trouble with both of you before, and as far as I can see, my best chance of clearing myself of the trouble you're tryin' to make for me, is by bringing in the murderers all tied up, and the only chance I've got of catching them and tieing them up and bringing them in is by staying as far away as possible from you and the police, because you'd only gum up the works.

Spade: You getting this all right, son, or am I goin' too fast for yuh?
Stenographer: No, sir. I'm getting it all right.
Spade: Good work.

Spade: Now, if you want to go to the board and tell them I'm obstructing justice and ask them to revoke my license, hop to it. Yuh tried it once before and it didn't get you anything but a good laugh ————all around.

Bryan: Now, look here.

Spade: And I don't want any more of these informal talks. I've nothing to say to you or the police, and I'm tired of being called things by every crack-pot on the city payroll, so if you want to see me, pinch me or subpoena me or something, and I'll come down with my lawyer.

Spade: I'll see you at the inquest, ————

Spade: maybe!

Wilmer: Come on, He wants to see you.

Spade: Well, I didn't expect you till five twenty-five. I hope I haven't kept you waiting.
Wilmer: Keep on ridin' me. They're gonna be pickin' iron out o' your liver!

Spade: The cheaper the crook, the gaudier the patter, huh? Well, let's go.

Spade: Come on. This'll put yuh in solid with your boss.

Gutman: Ah. Come in, sir. Thank you for coming. Come in.

Spade: Here. You shouldn't let him go around with those on 'im. He might get himself hurt.

Gutman: Well, well, what's this?

Spade: A crippled newsie took 'em away from him. I made him give 'em back.

Gutman: By gad, sir, you're a chap worth knowing. An amazing character. Gimme your hat.

Spade: Sit down there. I owe you an apology, sir.

Spade: Never mind that. Let's talk about the black bird.

Gutman: All right, sir, let's. Let's.

Gutman: This is going to be the most astounding thing you've ever heard of, sir, and I say this, knowing that a man of your caliber and your profession must have known some astounding things in his time.

Gutman: What do you know, sir, about the Order of the Hospital of Saint John of Jerusalem, later known as the Knights of Rhodes and other things?
Spade: Crusaders or something, weren't they?

Gutman: Very good. Sit down.

Gutman: In 1539, these Crusading Knights persuaded Emperor Charles the Fifth to give them the Island of Malta. He made but one condition.

Gutman: That they pay him each year the tribute of a falcon in acknowledgement that Malta was still under Spain.

Gutman: Do you follow me?
Spade: Uh-huh.

Gutman: Have you any conception of the extreme, the immeasurable wealth of the Order of that time?
Spade: I imagine they were pretty well fixed.

Gutman: Pretty well is putting it mildly. They were rolling in wealth, sir. For years they'd taken from the East, nobody knows what spoils of gems, precious metals, silks, ivory, sir.

Gutman: We all know the Holy Wars to them were largely a matter of loot. The Knights were profoundly grateful to the Emperor Charles for his generosity toward them. They hit upon the happy thought of sending him for his first year's tribute.

Gutman: Not an insignificant live bird but a glorious golden falcon crusted from head to foot with the finest jewels in their coffers. Well, sir, ——— what do you think of that?

Spade: I don't know.

Gutman: These are facts, historical facts; not school book history, not Mr. Wells's history, but history, nevertheless.

Gutman: They sent this foot-high jeweled bird to Charles who was then in Spain. They sent it in a galley commanded by a member of the Order. It never reached Spain. A famous admiral of buccaneers took the Knights' galley and the bird.

Gutman: In 1713 it turned up in Sicily.

Gutman: In 1840 it appeared in Paris. It had, by that time, acquired a coat of black enamel so that it looked nothing more than a fairly interesting black statuette.

Gutman: In that disguise, sir, it was as you may say, kicked around Paris for over three score years by private owners too stupid to see what it was under the skin.

Gutman: Then h'mm, in 1923 a Greek dealer named Charilaos Konstantinides found it in an obscure shop. No thickness of enamel could conceal value from his eyes.

Gutman: You begin to believe me a little?

Spade: I haven't said I didn't.

Gutman: Well, sir, to hold it safe while pursuing his researches into its history, Charliaos re-enamelled the bird. Despite this precaution, however, I got wind of his find. Ah, if I'd only known a few days sooner.

Gutman: I was in London when I heard. I packed a bag, got on the boat train immediately.

Gutman: On the train I opened a paper, the *Times*, and read that Charilaos's establishment had been burglarized and him murdered.

Gutman: Sure enough, on arriving there I discovered the bird was gone.

Gutman: That was seventeen years ago. Well, sir, it took me seventeen years to locate that bird, but I did. I wanted it! I'm a man not easily discouraged when I want something.

Gutman: I traced it to the home of a Russian general, ————

Gutman: ———— one Kemidov, in an Istambul suburb. He didn't know a thing about it. It was nothing but a black enamelled figure to him, but his natural contrariness kept him from selling it to me but I made him an offer.

Gutman: So I sent him some, er, agents to get it. Well, sir, they got it and I haven't got it, but I'm going to get it.

Gutman: Your glass.

Spade: Well, then, the bird doesn't really belong to any of you, but to a General Kemidov?

Gutman: Well sir, you might as well say it belonged to the King of Spain. I don't see how you can honestly grant anyone else a clear title to it, except by right of possession.

Gutman: And now, sir, before we start to talk prices.

Gutman: How soon can you, er, or how soon are you willing to produce the falcon?

Spade: A couple of days.
Gutman: That is satisfactory.

Gutman: Well, sir, here's to a fair bargain!

Gutman: Profits large enough for both of us!

Spade: What's your idea of a fair bargain?

Gutman: I will give you twenty-five thousand dollars when you deliver the falcon to me and another twenty-five thousand later on. Or, I will give you one quarter of what I realize on the falcon.

Gutman: That would amount to a vastly greater sum.
Spade: How much greater?

Gutman: Who knows? Shall we say a hundred thousand? Will you believe me if I name a sum that seems the probable minimum?

Spade: Why not?
Gutman: What would you say to a quarter of a million?

Spade: Then you think the dingus is worth a million, huh?

Gutman: In your own words, why not?
Spade: U'mm. That's a lot o' dough.

Spade: The minimum, huh? What's the maximum?
Gutman: The maximum I refuse to guess. You'd think me crazy. I don't know. There's no telling how high it could go, sir. That is the one and only truth about it! . . .

Gutman: Wilmer!

Spade: . . . Hello, Effie. It's me.
Effie: Yes, I know.
Spade: Let me talk to Miss O'Shaughnessy.

Spade: She isn't there? . . . What, she didn't show up?

Spade: Oh. Well, listen, you get on back to the office and wait there till I come or you hear from me. . . . Yeah, let's do something right for a change.

  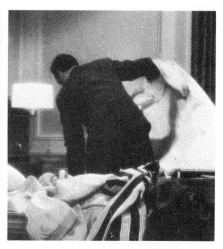

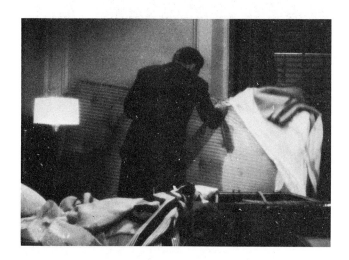 

SHIPPING NEWS

Arriving Today

5:35 P.M.—La Paloma from Hong Kong

6.20 P.M.—Shasta King from Seattle

8:45 P.M.—Tasmanian from Sydney and Hong

Mate: . . . It started in the hold aft, in the rear basement.
Reporter: What insurance was she carrying?

Man: Anybody burn?
2nd Man: No.
Man: Only the harbor watch was aboard!

Spade: . . . Someone I know came a———
Mate: What?
Spade: Someone I know came aboard this afternoon. I haven't seen her since. I'm worried.
Mate: No reason to be, mister. Everybody got off all right.

Spade: I wonder if you saw her. She's kinda small, about, er, five foot, er, ———
Mate: I couldn't, I couldn't tell yuh, mister. But if she came aboard she got off all right. Only the harbor watch was aboard when the fire started.

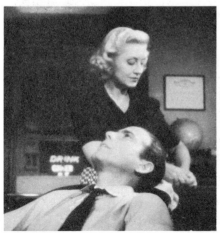

Spade: . . . Now you know as much about it as I do, precious. Maybe they went down to the ship. Maybe they didn't.

Effie: The part about the bird is thrilling.
Spade: Or ridiculous.

167

Jacoby: You know ———
Falcon ———

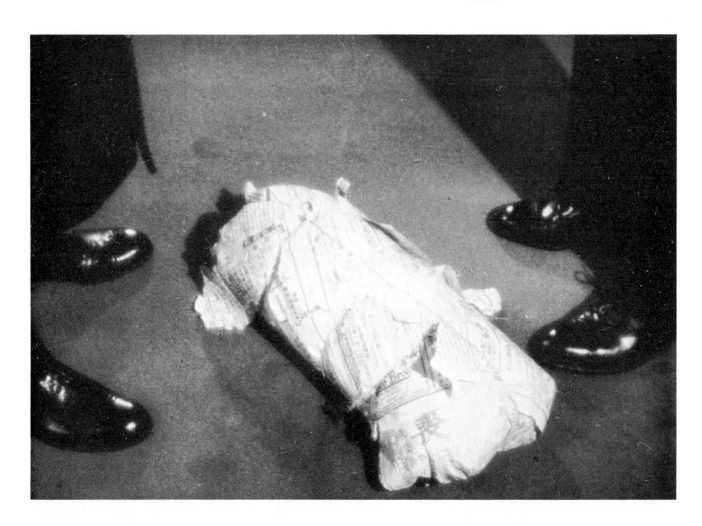

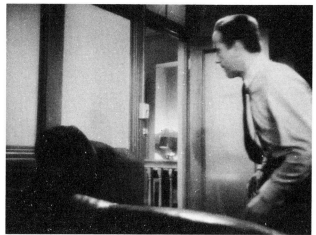

Spade: Lock that door.
Effie: . . . Is he, is he ———

Spade: Yeh. He couldn't have come far with those holes in 'em. . . .

Spade: Why couldn't he have stayed alive long enough to tell us something?

Spade: Here, here, here, none of that now. Come on. You can't pass out on me now.

Effie: All right, Sam . . . . Do you really think it's—

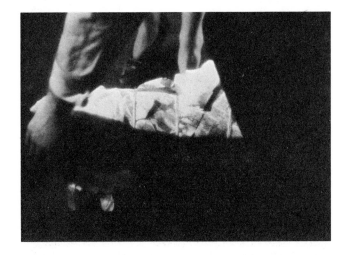 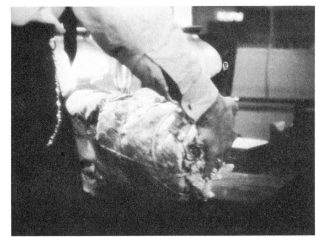

Spade: . . . We've got it, angel, we've got it.
Effie: You're hurting me.

Spade: Answer the phone.

Effie: Hello. . .Yes?. . .Who?. . . Oh, yes.

Effie: Where?. . . Yes, yes. . . Hello! Hello, hello!

Effie: It was Miss O'Shaughnessy! She wants you!
She's in danger!
Spade: Where is she?
Effie: Burlingame, Twenty-six Ancho. Oh, Sam,
her voice, it was awful!

Effie: Something happened to her before she
could finish. Go help her, Sam! Why, you've got
to go to her! Don't you see? He was helping
her and they killed him and ——— Oh,
you've got to go, Sam!

Spade: All right, I'll go! Now, after I've gone you phone the police. Tell 'em how it happened, but don't drag any names in!

Spade: You don't know. I got the phone call and I told you I had to go, but I didn't say where ———

Spade: Now, forget about this thing. Tell 'em how it happened, but without the bundle. Now, get that straight.

Spade Everything happened exactly as it did happen, but without the bundle and I got the phone call, not you ———
Effie: Yes, Sam.

Spade: Okay! . . . Shut this door and lock it behind me and don't open it till the police come ———

Effie: Oh! Do you know who he is?
Spade: Yeh! he's Captain Jacoby, master of the La Paloma. You're a good man, sister!

Spade: May I borrow your pencil?
Clerk: Sure!

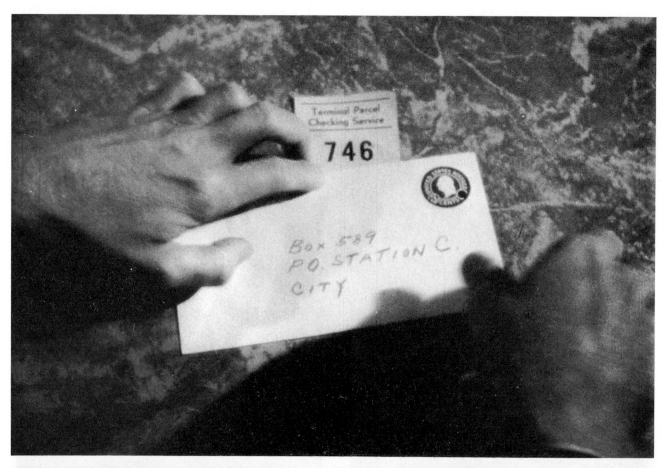

Spade: Say Frank?

Frank: Oh, hello, Mr. Spade.
Spade: You got plenty of gas?
Frank: Sure thing.

Spade: Do you know where Ancho Street or
Avenue is in Burlingame?
Frank: Nope. But if she's there we can find her.

Spade: Well, twenty-six is the number and the
sooner the better.
Frank: Correct!

Spade: Keep your motor running.

Frank: Bum steer, Mr. Spade?

Spade: Yeah. Let's get to a phone booth.

Spade: Thanks. Good night, Frank!
Frank: Good night.

Spade: Hello, Mrs. Perine? Effie there? Yes please . . .
Hello, precious! What's the good news? . . . No, no.
It was a bum steer. Are you sure that was her voice?
Well, it was hooey. Everything go all right? . . .
Nothing said about the bundle, huh? . . . That's
swell! Did they take you down to the hall? . . .Um-
huh, All right precious. You'd better hit the hay
and get a good night's rest. You sound all in. . . .
Oh, no. Save it till tomorrow. I'm going on home. . . .

Brigid: Mr. Spade! . . . I've been hiding in a doorway up the street. I thought you'd never come.

Spade: Can you make it all right or shall I carry yuh?

Brigid: I'll be all right as soon as I can get some place where I can lie down.

Gutman: Well, sir, we're all here. Now, let's come in and sit down and be comfortable and talk.
Spade: Sure.

Brigid: Oh!
Spade: Get away! You're not gonna frisk me.

Wilmer: Stand still! Shut up!
Spade: Take your paws off or I'll make yuh use that gun. Ask your boss if he wants me shot up before we talk.

Gutman: Never mind, Wilmer. You certainly are a most headstrong individual. Well, let's be seated.

Spade: Well, are you ready to make the first payment and take the falcon off my hands?

Gutman: Well, sir, as to that ———

Gutman: As to that.

Spade: Ten thousand? We were talkin' about a lot more money than this.

Gutman: Yes, sir, we were. But this is genuine coin of the realm. With a dollar of this you can buy ten dollars of talk.

Gutman: And there are more of us to be taken care of now.

Spade: Well, that may be, but I've got the falcon!

Cairo: I shouldn't think it would be necessary to remind you, Mr. Spade, that you may have the falcon, but we certainly have you.

Spade: Yeh, well, I'm tryin' not to let that worry me. We'll get back to the money later on. There's something else to be discussed first.

Spade: We've got to have a fall guy. The police have gotta have a victim.

Spade: Somebody they can pin those three murders on.

Cairo: Three? There's only two, because Thursby certainly killed your partner.

Spade: All right, only two then. What difference does it make? The point is, we've got to give the police ———

Gutman: Come, come, Mr. Spade, you can't expect us to believe at this late date that you're the least bit afraid of the police, or that you're not quite able to ———— handle ————

Spade: I'm in this up to my neck, Gutman.

Spade: I've got to find somebody, a victim when the time comes. If I don't I'll be it.

Spade: Let's give them the gunsel. He actually did shoot Thursby and Jacoby, didn't he?

Spade: Anyway he's made to order for the part. Look at him!

Spade: Let's give him to them.

Gutman: By gad, sir, you are a character. That you are!

Gutman: There's never any telling what you'll say or do next, except that it's bound to be something astonishing.

Spade: Why, it's our best bet. With him in their hands, the police will ———

Gutman: But, my dear man, can't you see that if I even for a moment thought of doing such a thing ——— That's ridiculous.

Gutman: I feel towards Wilmer, here, just exactly as if he were my own son. Really, I do. But if I even for a moment thought of doing what you propose.

Gutman: What in the world would keep Wilmer from telling the police every last detail about the falcon and all of us.

Spade: Let him talk his head off. I'll guarantee you nobody'll do anything about it.

Gutman: Well, well, what do you think of this, Wilmer?

Gutman: Mighty funny, eh?
Wilmer: Mighty funny.

Spade: How do you feel now? Any better, precious?

Brigid: Much better. But I'm frightened.
Spade: Well, don't be. Nothing very bad's going
to happen here. Do you want a drink, angel?

Brigid: Be careful, Sam.

Sam: Well ———

Gutman: If you're really serious about this, the
least we can do in common politeness is to hear
you out. Now, how would you be able to fix it ———

Gutman: ———— Hm-hm, hm

Gutman: ———— So that Wilmer couldn't do us any harm?

Spade: I can show Bryan, our district attorney, that if he goes around tryin' to collect everybody he's gonna have a tangled case.

Spade: But if he sticks to Wilmer here, he can get a conviction standing on his head.

Wilmer: Get up on your feet! I've taken all the riding from you I'm gonna take. Get up and shoot it out!

Spade: Young wild west!

Spade: Maybe you'd better tell him that shootin' me before you get your hands on the falcon's gonna be bad for business.
Gutman: Now, now, Wilmer. We can't have any of that. You shouldn't let yourself attach so much importance to these things.

Wilmer: Make him lay off me then.

Gutman: Now, Wilmer

Gutman: Your plan is, er, not at all satisfactory, sir. Let's not say anything more about it.

Spade: All right. I've got another suggestion. It may not be as good as the first one, but it's better than nothing. Do you want to hear it?

Gutman: Most assuredly.

Spade: Give them Cairo.

Gutman: H'mm. Well, by gad, sir.
Cairo: And suppose we give them you or Miss O'Shaughnessy? How about that, huh?

Spade: You want the falcon. I've got it! The fall guy's part of the price I'm asking.

Spade: As for Miss O'Shaughnessy, if you think she can be rigged for the part.

Spade: I'm perfectly willing to discuss it with you.

Cairo: You seem to forget that you are not in a position at all to insist upon anything.

Gutman: Now, come, gentlemen. Let's keep our discussion on a friendly basis. But, certainly, there's something in what Mr. Cairo said.

Spade: If you kill me, how are you gonna get the bird? And if I know you can't afford to kill me, how are you gonna scare me into giving it to you?

Gutman: Well, sir, there are other means of persuasion besides killing and threatening to kill.

Spade: Yes, that's ———— That's true. But there're none of them any good unless the threat of death is behind them.

Spade: Do you see what I mean. If you start something, I'll make it a matter of your having to kill me or call it off.

Gutman: That's an attitude, sir, that calls for the most delicate judgment on both sides. Because, as you know, sir, in the heat of action men are likely to forget where their best interests lie and let their emotions carry them away.

Spade: And the trick from my angle is to make my play strong enough to tie you up, but not make you mad enough to bump me off against your better judgment.

Gutman: By gad, sir, you are a character.

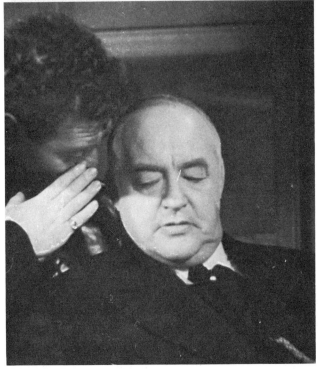

Spade: Six, two, and even, they're selling yuh out, sonny.

Spade: I hope you're not letting yourself be influenced by the guns these pocket edition desperadoes are waving around.

Spade: Because I've practised taking guns away from these boys before so we'll have no trouble there. Wilmer, here, is ———

Wilmer: All right ———
Gutman: Wilmer! Wilmer! Wilmer!

 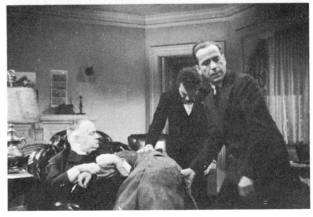

Spade: There's our fall guy. Now either you'll say yes right now or I'll turn the falcon and the whole lot of yuh in.

Gutman: I don't like that, sir.
Spade: Well, you won't like it. Well ———

Gutman: You can have him.

Spade: I won't be able to get the falcon till daylight, and maybe later.

Gutman: It strikes me that it'd be best for all concerned, if we did not get out of each other's sight until our business has been transacted. You have the envelope.

Spade: Miss O'Shaughnessy has it. That's all right. Hang on to it.

198

Spade: We don't have to lose sight of each other. The dingus'll be brought to us here.

Gutman: Excellent, sir, excellent! Then in exchange for the ten thousand and Wilmer, you will give us the falcon and an hour or two of grace!

Spade: Now, let's get the details fixed, first.

Spade: Why did he shoot Thursby and why and where and how did he shoot Captain Jacoby?

Spade: You see, I've got to know all that happened so I can be sure the parts that don't fit are covered up!

Gutman: I shall be candid with you, sir. Thursby was Miss O'Shaughnessy's ally. We believed that disposing of him in the manner we did ———

Gutman: Would cause Miss O'Shaughnessy to stop and think that perhaps it would be best to patch up her differences with us regarding the falcon.

Spade: Then you didn't try to make a deal with him before giving him the works?

Gutman: We did. Yes, sir. We certainly did. I talked to him, myself, that very night; but I could do nothing with him.

Gutman: He was quite determinedly loyal to Miss O'Shaughnessy.

Gutman: So Wilmer followed him back to the hotel and did what he did!

Spade: Aw, that sounds all right. Now, Jacoby ——

Gutman: Captain Jacoby's death was entirely Miss O'Shaughnessy's fault.
Spade: Tell me what happened.

Gutman: Well, Cairo, as you must have surmised, got in touch with me after he left police headquarters yesterday night or morning.

Spade: He recognized the mutual advantage of pooling forces. Mr. Cairo is a man of nice judgment.

Gutman: The Paloma was his thought. He saw the notice of its arrival in the papers and remembered that he had heard in Hong Kong that ———

202

Gutman: Jacoby and Miss O'Shaughnessy were seen together.

Gutman: Well, sir, he saw that and, putting two and two together, guessed the truth. She'd given the bird to Jacoby to bring here for her.

Spade: And at that juncture, you decided to slip me a mickey, huh?

Gutman: There's no place for you in our plan, sir.

Gutman: So we decided to spare ourselves any possible embarrassment. Mr. Cairo and Wilmer and I went to call on Captain Jacoby.

Gutman: We were lucky enough to arrive while Miss O'Shaughnessy was there. In many ways, the conference was difficult, but we finally persuaded Miss O'Shaughnessy to come to terms, or so we thought.

Gutman: We then left the boat and set out for my hotel, where I was to pay Miss O'Shaughnessy and receive the bird.

Gutman: Well, sir, we mere men should have known better. En route, she, Captain Jacoby and the falcon slipped completely through our fingers.

Gutman: It was nicely done, sir. Indeed, it was.

Spade: You touched off the boat before you left?

Gutman: No, not intentionally. Though, I dare say we, or Wilmer at least, were responsible for the fire.

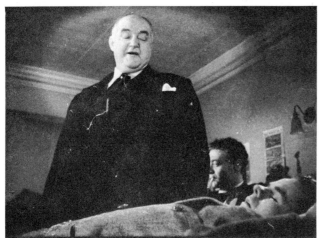

Gutman: While the rest of us were talking in the cabin, Wilmer went about the boat trying to find the falcon.

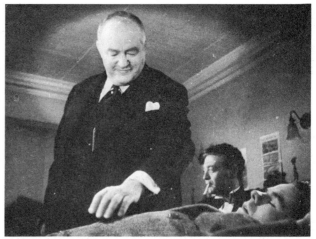

Gutman: No doubt, he was careless with matches.

Spade: Now, about the shooting?

Gutman: We caught up with Miss O'Shaughnessy and Jacoby at her apartment.

Gutman: I sent Wilmer downstairs to cover the fire escape before ringing the bell.

Gutman: And, sure enough while she was asking us who we were through the door and we were telling her, we heard a window go up.

Gutman: Wilmer shot Jacoby as he was coming down the fire escape; shot him more than once, but Jacoby was too tough to fall or drop the falcon. He climbed down the rest of the way, knocked Wilmer over, and ran off.

Gutman: We persuaded, that is the word, sir, ——— we, er, persuaded Miss O'Shaughnessy to tell us where she had Captain Jacoby take the falcon.

Gutman: And we, er, further persuaded her to phone your office, in an attempt to draw you away, before Jacoby got there, but, unfortunately for us, ———

Wilmer: Ohhhh!
Gutman: It had taken us too long to persuade Miss O'Shaughnessy. And you had the falcon before we could reach you.

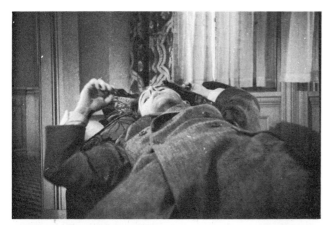

Gutman: Well, Wilmer, I'm sorry, indeed, to lose you, but I want you to know I couldn't be fonder of you if you were my own son.

Gutman: Well, if you lose a son it's possible to get another. There's only one Maltese falcon.

Gutman: When you're young, you simply don't understand these things.
Spade: How about some coffee?

Spade: Put the pot on, will you, angel? I don't like to leave our guests.
Brigid: Surely.

Gutman: Just a moment, my dear. Hadn't you better leave the envelope in here.

Brigid: Sit on it, if you're afraid of losing it.
Gutman: You misunderstand me.

Gutman: It's not that a'tall, but business should be transacted in a business-like manner.

Gutmann: For instance, there are only nine bills here now. There were ten when I handed them to you, as you very well know.

Spade: Well? I wanta know about this.

Spade: You palmed it?

Spade: Yes. Do you want to say so, or do you want to stand for a frisk?
Gutman: Stand for ———

Spade: You're going to admit it, or I'm gonna search yuh. There's no third way.
Gutman: By gad, sir, I believe you would. I really do. You are a character, if you don't mind my saying so.

Spade: You palmed it.

Gutman: Yes, sir, that I did.

Gutman: I must have my little joke now and then.

Gutman: And I was curious to know what you would do in a situation of this sort. I must say you passed the test with flying colors.

Spade: Ah! That's the sort of a thing I'd expect from somebody Wilmer's age.

Gutman: This will soon be yours. You might as well take it.

Spade: I oughta have more than ten thousand.
Gutman: of course, sir, you understand this is the first payment. Later.
Spade: Oh, yes. Later you'll give me millions, but, er, how's about fifteen thousand now?

Gutman: Frankly and candidly, upon my word of honor as a gentleman, ten thousand is all the money I can raise.

Spade: But you didn't say positively.

Gutman: Positively.

Gutman: I'd like to give you a word of advice.
Spade: Go ahead.

Gutman: I dare say you're going to give her some money, but if you don't give her as much as she thinks she ought to have, my word of advice is, be careful.

Spade: Dangerous?
Gutman: Very.

Spade: How's the coffee coming, angel?
Brigid: In a few minutes.

Gutman: It's almost daylight. Mr. Spade. Can you start getting it now?
Spade: I guess so.

Spade: Hello, precious, I'm sorry to get you up so early. Now, listen carefully. Here's the picture! In the Holland box, at the post office, there's an envelope with my scrawl. In that envelope, there's a parcel room check for the bundle we got yesterday . . . Oh-huh. Now, get that bundle and bring it here, P.D.Q. . . . Ah, that's a good girl. Now, hustle, good bye.

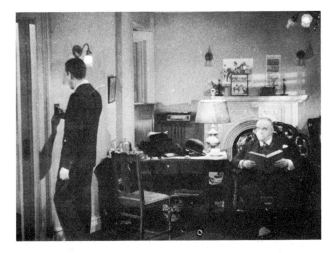

Spade: Thanks, lady. Sorry to spoil your day of rest.
Effie: Not the first one you've spoiled, anything else?

Spade: No. No, thanks.
Effie: Bye-bye, then.

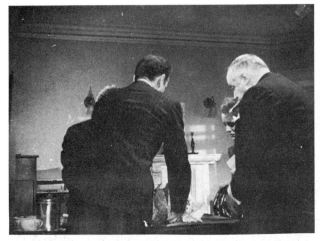

Spade: There you are.

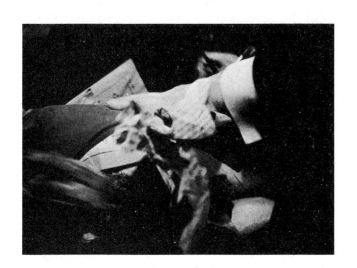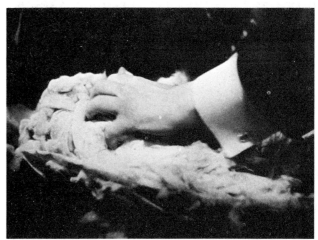

Gutman: Now, after seventeen years!

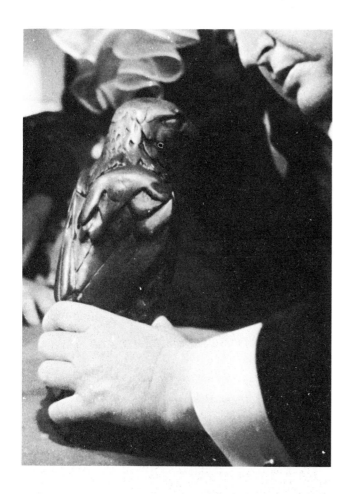 

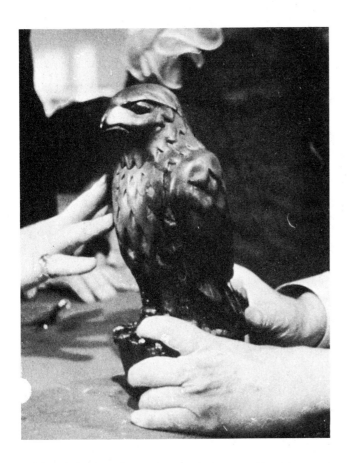 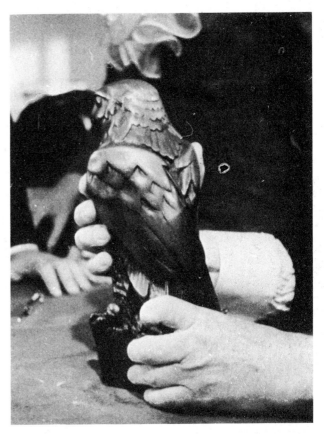

Gutman: It is it! But we'll make sure.

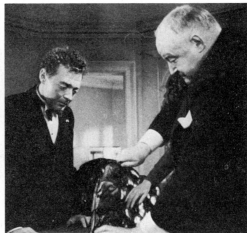

Gutman: Fake! It's a phoney!

Gutman: It — It's lead! It's lead! It's a fake!

Spade: All right, you've had your little joke. Now, tell us about it.

Brigid: No, Sam! No! That's the one I got from Kemidov. I swear it.

Cairo: You! It's you who bungled it! You and your stupid attempt to buy it!

Cairo: Kemidov found out how valuable it was! No wonder we had such an easy time stealing it!

Cairo: You — you imbecile! You bloated idiot!
You stupid fat-head, you!

Gutman: Yes, it's the Russian's hand. There's no doubt about it.

Gutman: Well, sir, what do you suggest, we stand here and shed tears and call each other names, or shall we go to Istanbul?

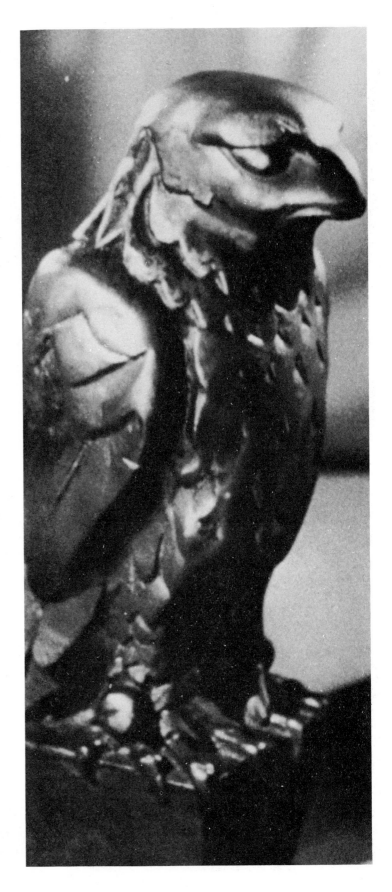

228

Cairo: Are you going?

Gutman: Seventeen years I've wanted that little item, and have been trying to get it.

Gutman: If we must spend another year on the quest, well, sir,

Gutman: It will be an additional expenditure in time of only five and fifteen-seventeen per cent.

Cairo: I'm going with you!

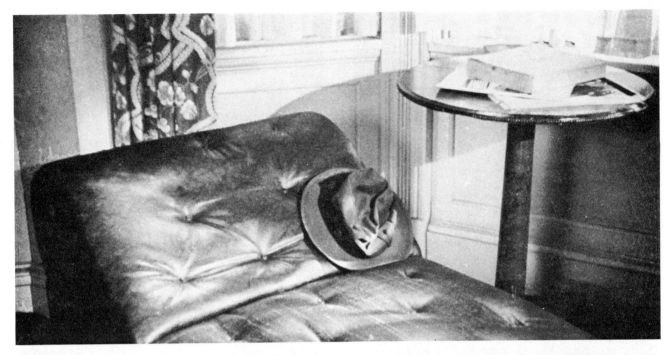

Gutman: Wilmer!

Spade: A swell lot o' thieves!

Gutman: We've little enough to boast about, sir, but the world hasn't come to an end just because we've run into a little set-back.

Gutman: I must ask you for that envelope.
Spade: I held up my end. You got your dingus. It's your hard luck, not mine, it wasn't what you wanted.

Gutman: Now, come, sir, we've all failed, and there's no reason for expecting any of us to bear the whole brunt.

Gutman: In short, sir, I must ask you for my ten thousand.

Spade: This'll take care of my time and expenses.

Gutman: Now, sir, we'll say goodbye to you, unless you care to undertake the Istanbul expedition with us. You don't?

Gutman: Well, frankly, sir, I'd like to have you along, you're a man of nice judgment and many resources.

Gutman: Now that there's no alternative, I dare say you'll manage the police without a fall guy.

Spade: I'll make out, all right.

Gutman: Well, sir, the shortest farewells are the best.

Gutman: Adieu. And to you, Miss O'Shaughnessy, I leave the Rara Avis on the table as a little momento.

Spade: Hello. Sergeant Polhaus there? . . . Yeah . . . Put him on . . . this is Sam Spade . . .

Hello. Tom? . . . Now, listen. I've got something for you. Here it is: Jacoby and Thursby were killed by a man named Wilmer Cook . . . Yeh. He's about twenty years old, five foot, six, wearing a gray overcoat. He's working for a man named Kasper . . . Gutman . . .Naa. You can't miss Gutman. He must weigh three hundred pounds. That fella Cairo's in with 'im, too. And they just left here for the Alexandria Hotel, but you'll have to move fast. They're blowing town. Now, watch yourself when you go up against the kid . . . Yes, that's right. Very. Well, good luck, Tom.

Spade: Now, they'll talk when they're nailed about us. We're sitting on dynamite. We've got only minutes to get set for the police. Now, give me all of it fast!

Spade: When you first came to my office, why did you want Thursby shadowed?

Brigid: I told you, Sam. I thought he was betraying me, and I wanted to find out.

Spade: That's a lie! You had Thursby hooked, and you know it, and you wanted to get rid of him before Jacoby came with the loot so you wouldn't have to split it with him.

Spade: Isn't that so? What was your scheme?

Brigid: I thought if he knew someone was following him, he'd be frightened into going away.

Spade: Miles wasn't clumsy enough to be spotted the first night. You told Thursby he was being followed.

Brigid: I told him. I told him.

Brigid: Yes, but, please believe me, Sam.

Brigid: I wouldn't have told him if I'd thought Floyd would kill him.

Spade: If you thought he wouldn't kill Miles, you were right, angel.

Spade: Miles hadn't many brains, but he'd had too many years of experience as a detective to be caught like that by a man he was shadowing up a blind alley with his gun in his hip and his overcoat buttoned.

Spade: But he'd have gone up there with you, angel. He was just dumb enough for that. He'd have looked up and down and licked his lips and gone, grinning from ear to ear.

Spade: And then you could have stood as close to him as you liked in the dark. And put a hole through him with a gun you got from Thursby that evening.

Brigid: Don't Sam! Don't say that! You know I didn't ———
Spade: Stop it! The police'll be here any minute! Now talk!

Brigid: Oh, why do you accuse me of such a ————
Spade: This isn't the time for that school girl act! We're both of us sitting under the gallows! Now, why did you shoot Miles?
Brigid: I didn't mean to at first, really, I didn't, but when I found out that Floyd couldn't be frightened, I ——— Oh, I can't look at you and tell you this, Sam!

Spade: You thought Thursby would tackle Miles and one or the other of them would go down. If Thursby was killed, you were rid of him.

Spade: It it was Miles, you'd see that Thursby was caught and sent up for it. Isn't that right?

Brigid: Something like that.

Spade: And when you found Thursby wasn't going to tackle him, you borrowed his gun and did it yourself! Right?

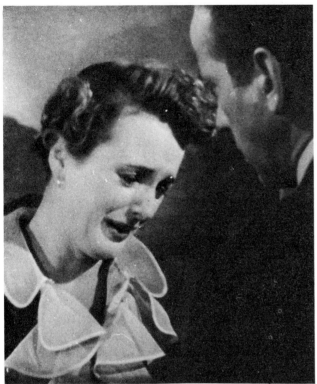

Spade: And when you heard Thursby was shot, you knew Gutman was in town! And you knew you needed another protector, somebody to fill Thursby's boots, so you came back to me.

Brigid: Yes! Oh, sweetheart, it wasn't only that! I'd have come back to you sooner or later. From the very first instant I saw you, I knew.

Spade: Well, if you get a good break, you'll be out of Tahatchapi in twenty years, and you can come back to me then.

Brigid: You're not ———

Brigid: Don't Sam! Don't say that, even in fun!

Spade: I hope they don't hang you, precious, by that sweet neck.

Spade: Yes, angel, I'm gonna send you over. The chances are you'll get off with life. That means if you're a good girl, you'll be out in twenty years. I'll be waiting for you. If they hang you, I'll always remember you.

Brigid: Oh, I was frightened for a minute. I really thought ——— You do such wild and unpredictable things.

Spade: Now, don't be silly. You're taking the fall.

Brigid: You've been playing with me; just pretending you cared, to trap me like this. You didn't care at all! You don't love me!

Spade: I won't play the sap for you!

Brigid: Oh, you know it's not like that! You can't say that!

Spade: You never played square with me for half an hour at a stretch since I've known yuh!

Brigid: You know, down deep in your heart that, in spite of anything I've done, I love you.

Spade: I don't care who loves who! I won't play the sap for you! I won't walk in Thursby's, and I don't know how many others footsteps!

Spade: You killed Miles and you're going over for it.
Brigid: Oh. How can you do this to me, Sam? Surely, Mr. Archer wasn't as much to you as ———

Spade: Listen. This won't do any good. You'll never understand me, but I'll try once and then give it up.

Spade: When a man's partner's killed, he's supposed to do something about it. It doesn't make any difference what you thought of him. He was your partner, and you're supposed to do something about it.

Spade: And it happens we're in the detective business. Well, when one of your organization gets killed, it's bad business to let the killer get away with it; bad all around; bad for every detective everywhere.

Brigid: You don't expect me to think that these things you're saying are sufficient reasons for sending me to the ————

Spade: Wait'll I'm through. Then, you can talk.

Spade: I've no earthly reason to think I can trust you.

Spade: And if I do this and get away with it, you'll have something on me that you can use whenever you want to.

Spade: Since I've got something on you, I couldn't be sure that you wouldn't put a hole in me some day.

Spade: All those are on one side.

Spade: Maybe some of them are unimportant. I won't argue about that. But look at the number of them. What have we got on the other side?

Spade: All we've got is that maybe you love me and maybe I love you.

Brigid: You know whether you love me or not.

Spade: Maybe I do. I'll have some rotten nights after I've sent you over, but that'll pass.

Spade: If all I've said doesn't mean anything to you, then forget it, and we'll make it just this.

Spade: I won't because all of me wants to, regardless of consequences, and because you've counted on that with me, the same as you counted on that with all the others.

Brigid: Would you have done this to me if the falcon had been real and you'd got your money?

Spade: Don't be too sure I'm as crooked as I'm supposed to be. That sort of reputation might be good business ———

Spade: Bringing high priced jobs and making it easier to deal with the enemy, but a lot more money would have been one more item on your side of the scales.

Brigid: If you'd loved me, you wouldn't have needed any more on that side.

Spade: Come in.

Spade: Hello, Tom.

Spade Got 'em?
Polhaus: Got 'em.

Spade: Swell! Here's another one for yuh.

Spade She killed Miles. Oh, and I've got some exhibits: the boys' guns, one of Cairo's, a thousand dollar bill I was supposed to be bribed with.

Spade: And this black statuette here that all the fuss was about.

Spade: What's the matter with your little playmate?

Spade: He looks broken-hearted. I bet when he heard Gutman's story, he thought he had me.

Polhaus: Cut it out, Sam.

Spade: Well, shall we be getting on down to the Hall?

Polhaus: It's heavy. What is it?

Spade: The, er, stuff that dreams are made of.

Polhaus: Huh?

The End

WB A WARNER BROS.
FIRST NATIONAL PICTURE

THE PLAYERS
Samuel Spade
  ... HUMPHREY BOGART
Brigid O'Shaughnessy
  ... MARY ASTOR
Iva Archer ... GLADYS GEORGE
Joel Cairo ..... PETER LORRE
Lt. of Detectives Dundy
  ... BARTON MacLANE
Effie Perine ..... LEE PATRICK

Kasper Gutman
  ... SYDNEY GREENSTREET
Detective Tom Polhaus .. WARD BOND
Miles Archer ... JEROME COWAN
Wilmer Cook ... ELISHA COOK, Jr.
Luke .... JAMES BURKE
Frank Richman ... MURRAY ALPER
Bryan .... JOHN HAMILTON